GUITAR SOLO

T0085266

Bossa, Samba & Tango Duets
FOR GUITAR and FLUTE
plus percussion

To access audio visit:
www.halleonard.com/mylibrary

Enter Code
7463-2856-1072-7564

ISBN 978-1-59615-731-6

 Music Minus One

EXCLUSIVELY DISTRIBUTED BY

HAL•LEONARD®

Visit Hal Leonard Online at
www.halleonard.com

Contact us:
Hal Leonard
7777 West Bluemound Road
Milwaukee, WI 53213
Email: info@halleonard.com

In Europe, contact:
Hal Leonard Europe Limited
42 Wigmore Street
Marylebone, London, W1U 2RN
Email: info@halleonardeurope.com

In Australia, contact:
Hal Leonard Australia Pty. Ltd.
4 Lentara Court
Cheltenham, Victoria, 3192 Australia
Email: info@halleonard.com.au

Christian Reichert

Christian Reichert shows a command of the guitar that encompasses both extreme sensitivity and virtuosity. The guitarist with "the fascinating technical experience and perfect rhythm" won several international prizes in Spain (Andrés Segovia International Guitar Competition), Poland, Bulgaria (International Guitar Foundation) and Germany. Since then the artist who "fills the audience easily with enthusiasm" (*El País*, Spain) concertizes and gives master classes frequently in the U.S. and other international venues, including Paris, Moscow, Granada, Montreux, Stockholm, Cracow, Sofia and Vienna.

Born in Würzburg, Germany, in 1971, he studied with Hans Koch and Johannes Tappert and at the Freiburg and Cologne academies with Sonja Prunnbauer and Argentinian master Roberto Aussel. During his studies he took part in master classes with such guitarists as Leo Brouwer, Manuel Barrueco, Roland Dyens, Sharon Isbin, Alvaro Pierri, Hubert Käppel and others. His interest in chamber music gave him the opportunity to play in a master class with the great singer Dietrich Fischer-Dieskau in Berlin. By age 21 he was a prize-winner at the Andrés Segovia International Guitar Competition in Granada, Spain. He won several prizes at the international competitions in Krynica, Cracow, Poland, and Frechen, Germany; and received a scholarship from the Richard Wagner Foundation in Bayreuth. In 1998 he received First Prize at the International Guitar Foundation's competition in Plovdiv, Bulgaria, as well as First Prize at the 1999 International Competition for Contemporary Music in Frankfurt together with flautist Katarzyna Bury.

Mr. Reichert is a frequent teacher of master classes and regularly performs as soloist and with all kinds of ensembles. Several composers have dedicated guitar works to him, and in addition to his much-lauded recordings for Music Minus One, he has recorded for many other labels and for many television and radio stations in Europe. In 2004 he began a CD-Guitar series for Waterpipe Records in Germany. If you'd like to learn more about this extraordinary artist, visit his website at *www.christianreichert.com*.

Katarzyna Bury

Polish-born flute virtuoso Katarzyna Bury has garnered acclaim wherever she performs. She studied at the music academies in Katowice with Prof. Ryszard Sojka and Prof. M. Katarzynski and also in Freiburg with Prof. Robert Aitken (Canada). She participated in many master classes with such world-famous artists as James Galway, Michel Debost, Eberhardt Grünenthal and others. While studying in Poland she had already become flutist with the Silesian Philharmonic Orchestra and was playing numerous concerts as a soloist in Poland and Germany. At nineteen years of age she was a prizewinner at the international flute competition in Krakow. She continued her studies in Germany, where she garnered further prizes at the international music competition *Pacem in terris* in Bayreuth and at the International Competition for Chamber Music in Frechen, together with guitarist Christian Reichert.

In 1999 Ms. Bury took the First Prize at the International Competition for Flute in Frankfurt. Together with guitarist Christian Reichert she has concertized extensively across Europe and won international chamber music prizes in Cologne and Frankfurt. In addition to her broad repertory, her interest in contemporary music is evident in her many performances of debut works. She has made numerous recordings for compact disc, radio and television and has performed many concerts as soloist and chamber musician both in Germany and abroad.

Music Minus One

3624

CONTENTS

Performance Notes for *Libertango* and *Granada*

The *tambora* technique on the beginning of Piazzolla´s famous *Libertango* is very common to us guitarists. Hit the strings with the thumb very close beside the bridge. If you want to improve this and bring out the upper line (here the high e-string) clearly, turn the right hand as much to the left until you hit the e-string with the nail part of the thumb. This will immediately give the upper line a proper accent and you can create a nice melody over the chords.

I use some *rasgueados* in *Granada* that are not very usual for a classical guitarist, but more flamenco-like. In bars 1-5, 17-21 and also 100-101, I play for every quarter-note eight sixty-fourth-notes. Here is the technique I use for these places: imagine that four sixty-fourth-notes are like one circle. I always start the circle with the thumb moving up (which means from the high strings to the low strings). The reason I start with the thumb is that it is the strongest finger, and so has to be the first of these four notes. The following three notes I do with the "a," "m" and "i" fingers in this order moving down (meaning from the low strings to the high strings). This should be practiced very slowly at the beginning and always having in mind that the right hand is not too tensioned and the moves are not too big. Only then can one make it to a proper speed.

Christian Reichert
Freiburg (Germany)
May 2006

LIBERTANGO

Arr. by Katarzyna Bury
and Christian Reichert

Astor Piazzolla

MMO 3624

SUITE POPULAR BRASILEIRA
(MUSIQUES POPULAIRES BRÉSILIENNES)

à Michel Caussanel

PAÇOCA (CHORO)

Celso Machado

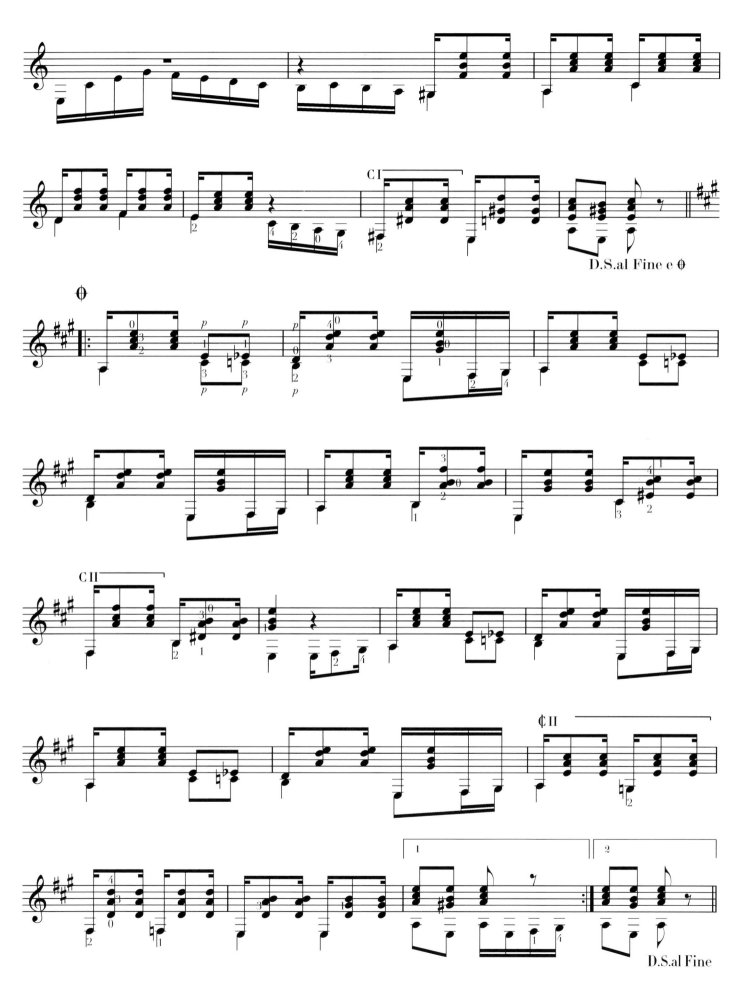

à Loredana Benvenuti

QUEBRA QUEIXO (CHORO)

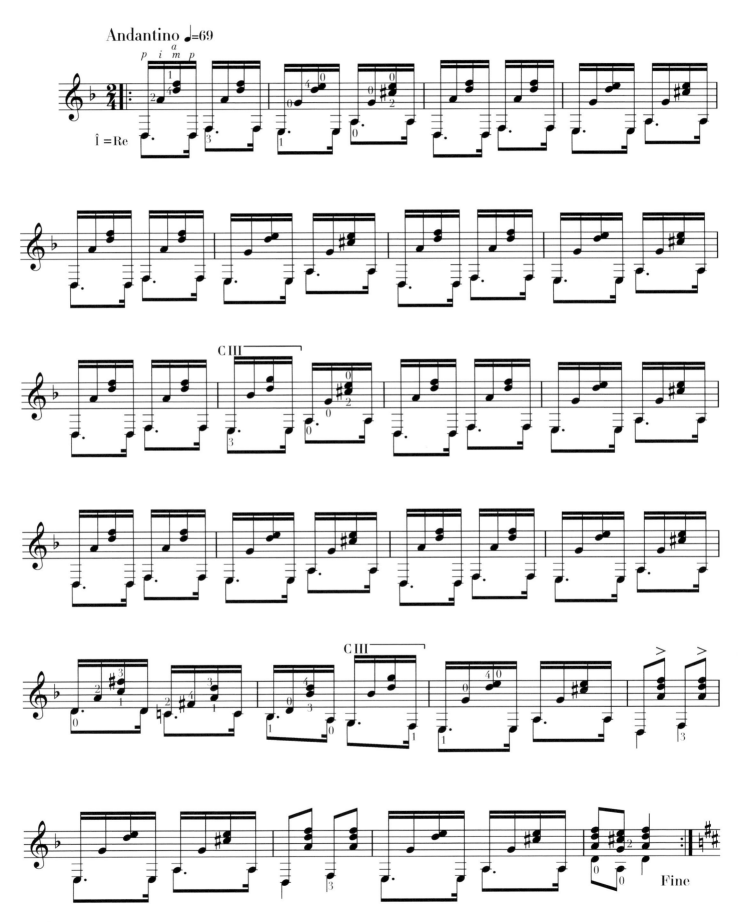

D.C.al ⊕ senza repet.

D.C.al Fine
senza repet.

à Ioria Agostini

PIAZZA VITTORIO (CHORO MAXIXE)

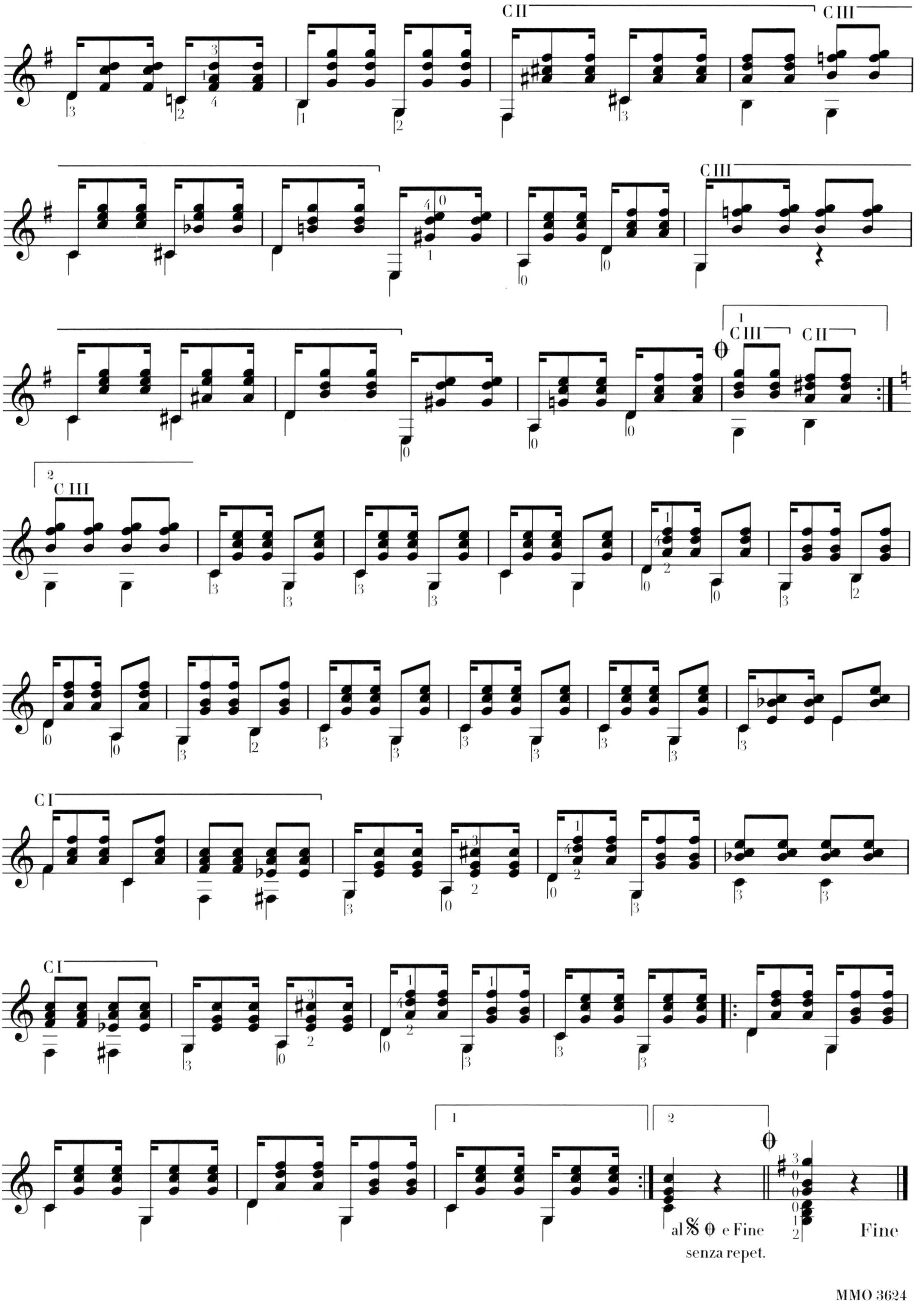
C II
C III
C III
C III
C II
C III
C I
C I
al 𝄋 Φ e Fine
senza repet.
Fine

à Thierry Rougier

ALGODÃO DOCE (SAMBA)

Fine

Rep. 4 times

à Franco Guidetti

SAMBOSSA (BOSSA NOVA)

D.C.al Θ e Fine

Fine

MMO 3624

pour Laura

PÉ DE MOLEQUE (SAMBA CHORO)

Fine

CARMEN-FANTAISIE

Arr. by Katarzyna Bury
and Christian Reichert

François Borne
(from George Bizet's Carmen*)*

HABANERA
Allegretto quasi Andantino

Variation II
Lento

Chanson de Bohème et Final

GRANADA

Arr. by Katarzyna Bury
and Christian Reichert

Augustín Lara